C000029208

Rea
....

Genesis 12–50

15 The Chambers, Vineyard
Abingdon OX14 3FE
brf.org.uk

Bible Reading Fellowship is a charity (233280)
and company limited by guarantee (301324),
registered in England and Wales

ISBN 978 0 85746 819 2
First published 2022
10 9 8 7 6 5 4 3 2 1 0
All rights reserved

Text © Richard S. Briggs 2020
This edition © Bible Reading Fellowship 2022
Cover illustration by Rebecca J Hall

The author asserts the moral right to be identified as the author of this work

Acknowledgements
Unless otherwise stated, scripture quotations are taken from The New Revised
Standard Version of the Bible, Anglicised edition, copyright © 1989, 1995 by
the Division of Christian Education of the National Council of the Churches of
Christ in the United States of America. Used by permission. All rights reserved.
• ESV: The Holy Bible, English Standard Version, published by HarperCollins
Publishers, © 2001 Crossway Bibles, a division of Good News Publishers. Used
by permission. All rights reserved. • NIV: The Holy Bible, New International
Version (Anglicised edition) copyright © 1979, 1984, 2011 by Biblica. Used
by permission of Hodder & Stoughton Publishers, a Hachette UK company.
All rights reserved. 'NIV' is a registered trademark of Biblica. UK trademark
number 1448790. • KJV: The Authorised Version of the Bible (The King
James Bible), the rights in which are vested in the Crown, are reproduced by
permission of the Crown's Patentee, Cambridge University Press. • MSG: *The
Message*, copyright © 1993, 1994, 1995, 1996, 2000, 2001, 2002 by Eugene H.
Peterson. Used by permission of NavPress. All rights reserved. Represented by
Tyndale House Publishers, Inc.

Every effort has been made to trace and contact copyright owners for material
used in this resource. We apologise for any inadvertent omissions or errors,
and would ask those concerned to contact us so that full acknowledgement
can be made in the future.

A catalogue record for this book is available from the British Library

Printed and bound by CPI Group (UK) Ltd, Croydon CR0 4YY

Genesis 12–50

Richard S. Briggs

Series editor: Simon P. Stocks

To my companions in Christian living at
St Mary's Sherburn – with thanks for sharing in
the joy of being part of God's church together.

I am grateful to Simon Stocks for the invitation
to write this little book, and to Melody Briggs
and Walter Moberly for their many helpful
comments on the text.

Each Really Useful Guide focuses on a specific
biblical book, making it come to life for the reader,
enabling them to understand the message and to
apply its truth to today's circumstances. Though
not a commentary, it gives valuable insight into
the book's message. Though not an introduction,
it summarises the important aspects of the book
to aid reading and application.

This Really Useful Guide to Genesis 12—50 will
transform your understanding of the biblical text,
and will help you to engage with the message in
new ways today, giving confidence in the Bible
and increasing faith in God.

Contents

1

Welcome to Genesis 12—50

A few years after I became a Christian, it occurred to me that I had never read through a whole book of the Bible – in one sitting – from beginning to end. I was reading the Bible a lot, but always in small sections and extracts. So early one morning, I sat in the corner of the kitchen, turned on a small table lamp in the darkness, opened my Bible to Genesis 1 and began reading. About two hours later, I closed the book at the end of Genesis 50, amazed at the story that had unfolded as I read.

It was like reading the world's first soap opera. After a most spectacular introduction, the story zoomed in on Abraham and his extended family, in and around what we call the 'ancient Near East'. So it seemed to me like 'ancient Near Eastenders'.

There were lovable heroes; unlovable heroes; twists and turns from joy to despair and back again; men and women praying and plotting, wheeling and dealing, weeping and dying. The key family seemed to be a strong candidate for the most dysfunctional of all time – buying and selling each other, lying about each other and leaving each other to desolation and even abuse. Yet they somehow stayed (more or less) together through it all. There were angels and visions, afternoon tea with God in person and a strange story about God (or was it an angel?) wrestling with Jacob through the night. At the end, there was even a long section that I recognised from singing in the choir of our school production of *Joseph and the Amazing Technicolour Dreamcoat*. By breakfast time, I had been to another world and back.

I actually learned two things from that journey. First, I learned that the best way to get to know a long Bible story is indeed to read it all the way through. Start by reading it as one long story, not getting stuck on all the details and questions it raises.

Second, I learned that the Bible can be treated well and with respect precisely by taking it as seriously as we take our favourite films and TV shows: by immersing ourselves in their worlds and letting the stories do their work on us. In other words, taking the Bible seriously involves using our imagination. You cannot enjoy a film when you interrupt it every few minutes to ask, 'How did they do that?' or 'Who is the guy in the corner with the camel?' Once you know and love the film, those questions make more sense. Likewise, once you know and love Genesis, those kinds of detailed questions have an important place. But first, you have to let your imagination run with the story. You have to jump in and hear and see it playing out on its own wide-screen terms.

This Really Useful Guide to Genesis 12—50 aims to get you up and running with enjoying the story, and then it looks at some interesting questions to ask about it. It is a guide to what you might do with this great big family drama that takes up most of the first book of our Bibles. How can you read it wisely and know what to look out for?

Most of all, I hope that you will end up on the same journey that I took one morning all those years ago, before breakfast, in the semi-darkness, watching a world – our world – take shape. Do you think that God knew that the best way to open up the Bible was with a fascinating story about men and women of faith and all their ups and downs?

Before we go any further...

Stop and read Genesis! Do what I did that morning in my kitchen. Get hold of a Bible, find a couple of hours with no phone or interruptions (breakfast is optional), and sit down and read it all the way through.

By the way, it really does not matter which translation you choose. There are a lot of different well-known Bible translations available (since Genesis, like most of the Old Testament, was originally written in ancient Hebrew). I quote from the New Revised Standard Version (NRSV). The most important thing is that you have a clearly printed Bible – and don't get distracted by notes or links to other things worth knowing about. Enjoy your reading.

2

What is Genesis 12—50?

Genesis 12—50 is not actually a book in itself. It is part of a longer book – Genesis – which is in turn part of a series of five books. This series is often called either the Books of Moses or the Pentateuch, which means 'five books'. The Pentateuch is in turn part of a longer collection: the whole Bible. In the Jewish faith, these five books have a special importance as the foundation of Jewish scripture. In the Christian faith, they remain in first place, as part of the Old Testament, in a Bible that goes on to also include the New Testament. Do Jews and Christians read Genesis the same way? Yes and no. It is the same book, but in different contexts. We will look out for examples of what difference this makes as we go on.

Sometimes I am going to cheat and call Genesis 12—50 a book. Although Genesis tells one continuous story from chapter 1 through to chapter 50, there is an important change of pace and focus at the beginning of chapter 12. Suddenly, we are looking in detail at one person, Abraham, and what happened to his family over several years. According to Genesis 11:10–26, Abraham was the latest in a long line of descendants that goes back to the sons of Noah, and before that all the way to Adam. So Genesis 12 is in one way simply the next part of the story.

But readers of Genesis have always noticed that there is this major change at chapter 12. So for practical purposes, we have divided our Really Useful Guide to Genesis into two separate guides, and you should consult the Genesis 1—11 guide for those chapters.

At the other end of the story, Genesis 50 both is and is not a conclusion. It does wrap up the stories of Jacob, who is Abraham's grandson, and Joseph, Abraham's great-grandson. This is not really followed up any further in the Bible, so there is a kind of ending here. Turn the page to Exodus 1 and we find a kind of new beginning. Now there is a new pharaoh in Egypt 'who did not know Joseph' (Exodus 1:8), and we are into the story of Moses. This new beginning is more like a new season of a TV drama, rather than a completely new show. For example, it is like *Doctor Who* with a new Doctor.

So it is useful to think of Genesis 12—50 as a book, as long as you remember that it is actually an episode (or a whole series of episodes) in a longer-running drama.

3

Who's who? Learning our way around Genesis 12—50

Genesis 12—50 is about people. It is also about God, but we will come on to that later. Who exactly are the people it is about?

I have a confession: I am terrible with names. My method of getting to grips with who's who in families is to draw a family tree. So let's do that.

Since Genesis does not actually set out to give us a family tree, there is more than one way to do it. Sometimes Genesis does list whole sections of family trees, or 'genealogies' as they are known, in ways that can feel a bit random. As a result, sometimes we have too much information, because if we included everyone it would get in the way of seeing how the family tree fits together. So what we need is a simplified outline of the major figures, a 'Who's who?' of key characters in the book. You may find it helpful to refer back to this diagram as you read the story for yourself:

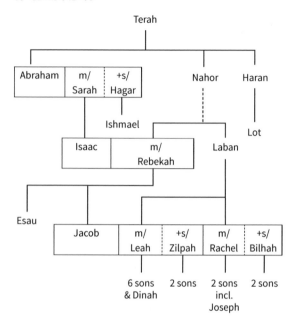

Key: m/ = married to; +s/ = also had children with wife's servant

Fig. 1: Abraham's family tree

I have included Terah here, because his descendants include more than just Abraham. But in terms of the actual story told in Genesis 12—50, we are looking at four generations. The key branch to notice is the line from Abraham to his son Isaac, then to his son Jacob and then to his son Joseph. Check that you can find this on the diagram.

We can call the overall story of Genesis 12—50 the 'ancestral narratives': stories of the ancestors of our faith. Unexpectedly for this ancient book, the focus is not just on the men. Key women play an essential role in the story. However, the ancient world usually told family stories in terms of the men first, which is why we know more about the male descendants in general.

These stories are relevant to us partly because they talk about an ancient part of our own family tree. We will see in a moment how these are *our* fathers and mothers, or ancestors. Likewise, in the Old Testament the word for 'father' can mean someone several generations back in the family tree, as well as someone's immediate father.

Clearly certain key figures are much more important than others in the story. Our 39 chapters can approximately be divided into three main episodes:

- Abraham and Sarah
- Jacob and his extended family troubles
- Joseph (and his amazing coat… and much else besides).

If Genesis 12—50 were a film series, it would probably be a trilogy. Most likely Isaac would not get a film to himself, although he would have several starring moments in the first two films.

I hope you find the family-tree approach helpful. The book of Genesis actually offers its own set of phrases that also organise the story for us. It often says, 'These are the generations of X', with X usually being a key figure. The word 'generations' comes from a Hebrew verb meaning 'to give birth to' (or 'to beget', as it was once translated). The phrase 'generations of X' could mean 'the family line of X' or even 'the stories of X'. The NRSV often translates it 'the descendants of X'. Whatever its precise meaning, the phrase occurs twelve times in the first few books of the Bible, almost all in Genesis.

Twelve is often a symbolic and important number in the Old Testament, so perhaps this is significant. Here is a complete list of them. Look out for this phrase as you read through Genesis yourself:

These are the generations of…

1 the heavens and the earth (2:4)
2 Adam (5:1)
3 Noah (6:9)
4 Noah's sons (Shem, Ham and Japheth) (10:1)
5 Shem (11:10)
6 Terah (11:27)
7 Ishmael, Abraham's son (25:12)
8 Isaac, Abraham's son (25:19)
9 Esau, that is, Edom (36:1)
10 Esau (36:9) – again!
11 the family of Jacob (37:2)
12 Aaron and Moses (Numbers 3:1).

You will notice that this list does not divide Genesis 12—50 up into sections of equal length. Basically, it separates out the Abraham and Sarah stories (up to chapter 25), the Jacob stories and then the whole Joseph narrative. This is the three-part summary I suggested earlier. Nobody knows why Abraham does not get his own heading or why Esau gets two. Overall, however, we can see clearly how focused Genesis 12—50 is on people, and people in one extended family in particular.

The bigger picture: 'Father Abraham'

Both Jews and Christians place Abraham's family tree in an even bigger family tree, to show that it is their own story being told. I remember singing a fun song in a youth group at church that began, 'Father Abraham had many sons / Many sons had Father Abraham.' It was an action song, so was always popular with children of all ages, at least up to embarrassed teenagers. It captures well the sense of being part of Abraham's family that is important to Christians, as well as to Jews.

The Old Testament includes a lot of family lists because it mattered who was related to who. Your identity was all about your family connections. Although not the most exciting to read, 1 Chronicles 1—9 lays out a vast family tree that includes the Abraham section (1 Chronicles 1:28–37; 2:1–4). If you look at 1 Chronicles 2:1–15 you will see how this then goes on to include the great king David.

The New Testament goes further and places all these family trees together in one picture that shows that Jesus comes from the line of David, and further back that he is a descendant of Abraham. This is clearest in

Matthew 1:2–16, though you can also see it, in reverse order, in Luke 3:23–38.

For Jews and for Christians, therefore, Abraham is our ancestor. For Jews this is through Abraham's actual family line, and for Christians it is by being brought into the family through Jesus. Whether we are Jew or Christian, Genesis 12—50 is part of our story. We are the children of 'Father Abraham'.

A note on names

As you read Genesis, you will realise that some characters change their names. On the whole this is not confusing, because the changes are recognisable:

- Abram becomes Abraham (17:5)
- Sarai becomes Sarah (17:15).

But sometimes it is more complicated:

- Jacob becomes Israel (32:28 and also 35:10)
- Joseph is called Zaphenath-paneah by Pharaoh (41:45), although it does not get used as his name again in the Bible.

We will think about these name changes when they come up. In this guide I take the simplest option and always use the most famous version of the person's name throughout, even when it is not strictly the version used in the story we are looking at.

4

A literary masterpiece: reading Genesis 12—50 at face value

What did you notice when you read through Genesis 12—50? Let's look at some key issues and themes that are part of the picture painted by the book. We are not going to ask historical questions here about what events took place all those centuries ago, or why Genesis tells this particular set of stories out of all the stories it might have told. Instead, we will aim to experience it as a dramatic story.

Let's take that journey I mentioned earlier, to the world found within the pages of Genesis. If you sit in the front row, popcorn in hand, and let the story of Genesis unfold, what strikes you? First, I will offer a brief guided tour of the whole story. Then we will look at some of the remarkable ways it tells us about the people at the centre of it – some of the people we just met in our 'Who's who?' section.

Keep your Bible open in front of you and use this next section to look again through the pages of Genesis as we go.

An overall read-through

In chapter 12, God says to Abraham, 'Get up and go!' Where? To the land that God will show him. And so he goes. This is a model of faithful obedience, stepping boldly into an unknown future. It comes with the promise of land, offspring (descendants) and great blessing. But it does not start well, and it does not start by showing those positive promises working out. First up, Abraham does not like the look of things in Egypt. It turns out later that many of Abraham's descendants will not like the look of things in Egypt. Abraham's bright idea is to ask his wife, his half-sister Sarah, to pass herself off as his sister. This does not go well for Pharaoh, or indeed for anybody.

In chapter 13, Abraham and Lot separate. They choose different lands to settle in. Lot chooses Sodom, which at the time was a thriving farmland. A strange chapter follows about foreign kings, wars and rumours of wars. Also a priest-king called Melchizedek, king of Salem (14:18), which will turn out to be Jerusalem eventually (see Psalm 76:2). Melchizedek blesses Abraham. His one brief appearance here gets remembered several times in the Bible (in Psalms and in Hebrews).

God makes a covenant with Abraham. A covenant is a solemn and binding agreement. We will explore covenants more carefully in chapter 5. For now, simply notice that God does this twice (in chapters 15 and 17). Do you think these chapters are telling about two different covenants or are they two versions of the same story, to emphasise its importance? It seems hard to tell. God promises to make Abraham's descendants numerous: more than the stars in the sky (15:5) or than the sand on the seashore (22:17). The only catch is that Abraham and Sarah have no children yet (16:1).

Sarah decides to try to fix this problem by giving her slave-girl Hagar to Abraham to have a child. Hagar duly gets pregnant, but unsurprisingly this creates huge friction in the family unit. A resentful Sarah sends Hagar away to die (chapter 16), although an angel saves her. Sarah also laughs when another angel repeats the promise of offspring (18:9–15). This is during a visit of three strangers to Abraham's tent, which develops into an unexpected encounter between Abraham and God about how many righteous people are needed to save Sodom from judgement. Abraham is concerned because his nephew Lot lives there, and in chapter 19 the sad tale of judgement plays out, although Lot is saved.

Time for Abraham to pretend his wife is his sister again. So he does that (chapter 20). It still goes badly. But God does give Sarah the long-awaited promised child: Isaac (21:1–3). Again Hagar is sent away, this time with her son Ishmael, and this time by Abraham, but not without a promise of their own, that they too will become a nation (21:13). In time, this will become part of the story of the Islamic faith and its own tradition.

God asks Abraham to sacrifice Isaac – even though he is the long-promised son (chapter 22). This is a story we will look at later. The sacrifice is averted, but we are told immediately that Sarah dies (23:1). Some say she died of a broken heart – what do you think? The new question of where to bury the faithful dead prompts Abraham to buy a field (chapter 23). And, mindful of advancing years, he asks a servant to sort out a wife for Isaac. The place to meet women in those days was at the well, since it was the women who had the job of fetching the water. So we literally have a kind of 'water-cooler moment'! The first of the Bible's great 'meeting with a woman at a well' stories takes place in chapter 24. Isaac marries Rebekah, and they live uneasily ever after. Abraham dies (25:1–11). What has Isaac learned from him? According to chapter 26, he has learned how to pretend his wife is his sister (26:7). So he does that.

By now, Isaac is old and he cannot see too well. Seeking to bless his older son Esau, he is tricked by Rebekah, who dresses up his younger son Jacob in hairy animal skins to look and smell more like Esau. Rebekah has had a word from the Lord, when she was pregnant, that the older son will serve the younger one (25:23), and so this story feels like Rebekah making sure it happens. Does that make a difference to who you have sympathy with as you read chapter 27? Isaac blesses the 'wrong' son, the younger one, Rebekah's favourite. It turns out that you cannot undo a blessing. Although that is hard on Esau, for most of us, most of the time, it is good news.

The family starts to disintegrate, and Jacob heads out, only to meet with God powerfully in a dream at Bethel (28:10–16). For all his failings and trickery, he prays a powerful prayer of hope for restoration to his father's house (28:21). But it takes a while for this to come about. First, he meets a woman at a well (of course). She turns out to be Rachel, the daughter of his uncle Laban (29:10), and he sets his heart on marrying her. (You might want to check back to the family tree if this is starting to sound confusing.) After quite some wedding night, he discovers in the morning that he has actually been fooled into marrying Rachel's sister Leah instead (29:25). The trickster has been tricked. He works for Laban seven years to earn the right to marry Rachel as well. We have another family set-up full of tension, bitter infighting and frustration over who will bear children. Not for want of trying, though: Jacob ends up with ten children through Leah, Leah's maidservant and Rachel's maidservant. Finally, Rachel conceives (30:22) and gives birth to Joseph. She eventually dies giving birth to Benjamin (35:18), son number twelve.

Meanwhile chapters 30—31 tell stories of Jacob's disorganised family life, his wheeling and dealing with Uncle Laban, always to his own advantage, and eventually the decision to flee and head back to the family home to meet brother Esau. Laban tries to follow Jacob and sort out the issues, which fails, although an uneasy peace is made.

Nervous about the imminent homecoming, Jacob sends everyone on ahead and waits in the middle of the night by a stream at Jabbok (32:22–32). The most extraordinary wrestling match takes place. Who is it who struggles with Jacob? Read the story and see if you can work it out. Is it even God himself? We will look at this in more detail later. Jacob is renamed Israel (32:28). Maybe it will be Israel's destiny to wrestle with God in the long centuries to come.

Perhaps older and wiser after his wrestling match with God, Jacob reunites with Esau in another moving moment of reconciliation, or at least a halting of hostilities (chapter 33). He becomes the grand old man of the rest of the book. From here on, the stories start to splinter into explorations of the deep problems arising in the extended family. We will look at some of these details later. As you read through, did you notice the two deeply distressing stories about the terrible treatment of women? Dinah, Leah's daughter, is raped in chapter 34, and Tamar, Judah's daughter-in-law, is also treated shamefully in chapter 38. How did you respond to those chapters?

We also encounter some long lists that keep track of who is related to who (especially chapter 36).

Then the teenager Joseph sits down and has a dream about being in charge of all his brothers (chapter 37). Look at 37:3 to see something about the family dynamics around Joseph. None of this goes down well with the brothers, and this leads to the extended story about Joseph in Egypt, which takes up a remarkable amount of space in the book. When Joseph and his brothers are finally reunited, after ten long chapters (enough to fill a two-hour musical), old man Jacob prays some prayers of blessing over his sons (chapters 48—49). Can you find here another example of mixing up which son gets which blessing? As you read these chapters, does it feel like you are watching the twelve sons of Jacob turning into the twelve tribes of Israel?

Jacob dies. Joseph runs the country. Joseph dies. The end.

In fact, the end of the book sees God's great promise of land and offspring precariously reduced to Joseph's bones in a box in the land of Egypt (50:26). Getting out of Egypt, and back on track with the big story, will take a hard struggle and a long journey to enter the promised land, as told in the following books of the Bible. Have a look at Joshua 24:32 for a final comment on the resting place of the bones of Joseph.

Stories about people

We have said that the book is all about people, and we mapped out a family tree of who they are. We have just recounted the outline of their stories. But what kind of people are they?

They live in an ancient world, with different customs from modern western readers. So some of what they do is unfamiliar to us. The stories assume a world of polygamy (having several wives), concubines (a woman in relationship with a man but with a lower status than a wife) and slavery. For example, when Abraham buys a field (chapter 23), we see a classic form of ancient eastern bargaining over a proper price that preserves honour and rights. The chapter begins with Abraham's wife Sarah dying. This prompts Abraham to reflect that he owns no land for burying his dead. The Hittites appear willing to give him land, but instead he insists on paying for it. Eventually, he is able to bury Sarah on his own land (23:19–20). Because he paid for it, the land is rightfully his – so he needed to reject what looked like a generous offer from the Hittites.

Such cultural details are important, but they are not the reason the story is told. They are important to us as readers, to help us follow the story better. But to people in the ancient world, none of these cultural features would have stood out. So a more interesting question is: what sort of people – what kind of characters – are we meeting as we read this story?

Heroes and villains? Or men and women like us?

You will notice as you read Genesis that there are very few moments when the narrator steps in and evaluates. In other words, there is no end-of-the-sermon moral added to the stories with statements like, 'So you see, brothers and sisters, we should learn not to do what Abraham did here.' Think back: did you find *any* examples of this as you read?

This absence is true of most of the Old Testament, in fact. The stories are told and left to do their work. This leaves us some room to ask the question, as we read, about whether we are reading a good example or a bad example of how to live for God.

A traditional view is that Abraham and co were 'heroes of the faith'. There is not really a biblical word for 'hero' (the nearest is 'mighty one/warrior'). But the idea partly comes from the list of great figures of faith in Hebrews 11, 'all… commended for their faith' (Hebrews 11:39). Take a look at Hebrews 11:8–22 for a short summary of some high points of the narrative of Genesis 12—50. Whose faith in particular does Hebrews pick out as being admirable?

It does make sense to say that the stories in Genesis 12—50 are designed to give us pictures of great people to learn from. Most Bible stories about men and women of faith can inspire us in one way or another to live for God. Given all that they were up against, Abraham and his descendants did a remarkable job of living by faith. Paul and others in the New Testament often point to Abraham for just this reason: he was not righteous because he followed the law (the law had not been given yet) but because he lived by faith. Paul found this a helpful counterbalance against those who said that pleasing God was all a matter of following the law.

Careful readers have pointed out, however, that a lot of what Abraham and co get up to in these stories is not straightforwardly good. Even on a quick readthrough, we see stories where:

- Abraham pretends his wife is his sister.
- Lot offers his daughters to a violent group attacking his house.
- Rebekah encourages one of her sons to cheat her other son out of his blessing, fooling her husband in the process.
- Laban tricks his nephew into marrying the wrong one of his daughters.

Clearly there are some complications with reading Genesis for examples of good behaviour to emulate.

So another common approach to the narratives of Genesis 12—50 is to say that God uses and blesses people like Abraham and co *even though they are particularly unworthy*. We could draw an encouraging lesson from this: if God can use such troublesome characters as these, then surely God can use us too. Again, there is some value in this approach, which like the 'heroes' approach does pick up on some details in the stories themselves. But maybe it is only because we expect them, as Bible characters, to be more like heroes that we can end up judging them so negatively.

Think now about how you apply God's standards to people that you know, such as Christian leaders or even yourself. Do you expect anyone to be always right or always wrong?

It makes more sense to suggest that we need both these pictures together to get the whole story. The main characters in Genesis 12—50 almost all have a mix of positive and negative characteristics. They perform acts of faith and bravery right alongside acts of deception and selfishness. In this, they are much like all God's people. So there is a time to honour them for their faith and a time to take a step back from their failings and think twice before copying them. In short: they are women and men of God... just like us.

In some ways all the points that we are about to look at in the rest of this section follow from this first one: that the people at the heart of the book's stories are neither especially heroes nor villains, but they show signs of the same mixture of good and bad actions and characteristics that you and I have. This makes the stories more relevant to all of us, in the end, whatever our culture and background. The men and women of Genesis offer us examples of the mixed life experience we all encounter – and maybe this was one reason why these stories were told in the first place. They teach us what faith looks like without editing out the difficult bits.

People who are learning to repair broken relationships

Not to set the bar particularly high, Genesis 12—50 shows us ways that family members learn to struggle through their differences without killing each other. They run it close a few times:

- Sarah sends Hagar away, unconcerned that she is more likely to die than anything else (21:10).
- Abraham sets out to sacrifice Isaac (22:1–3).
- Esau declares that he will kill his brother Jacob after Jacob has stolen his blessing (27:41).
- Joseph's brothers plot to leave him for dead (37:18–20).

But after Cain killed Abel in Genesis 4 (see the Really Useful Guide on Genesis 1–11), the whole unfolding tale sees people manage *not* to kill each other despite repeated breakdowns in family relationships.

It may be tempting for us to say, 'That's not very impressive. Is that the best the Bible can offer – that sometimes we manage not to kill each other?' But recall our emphasis on the good and bad in all these characters, and note the realistic portrait of extended family life as full of occasions for anger and mistrust.

Stories that are set out in this way speak to us of our own anger and our own experience of broken relationships. Genesis 12—50 speaks truthfully; sometimes, even in a family of great faith, relationships do break down.

When this happens, the response is not to dwell on the failure. For various reasons, Genesis spends very little time with people looking back over what they have done and talking about what went wrong. The focus is more on finding ways ahead and looking to how God leads people forward. As you saw when you read through the book, even the most troubled characters are capable of moments of humility, faithfulness and restoration of relationships. Look at how Jacob's moving prayer (28:20–21) leads on to a peaceful period when he finds a woman to marry. Then, even when he is tricked into marrying the wrong woman, he simply commits to further years of work to earn the right one as well (29:27–28). And yet in his ongoing relationships with Laban, there remains selfishness and distrust, up until Laban agrees a kind of truce with him. Look at 31:51–54 to see what sort of resolution they manage.

There is not much evidence of people ever actually forgiving each other in Genesis. Esau seems to treat Jacob generously when they reunite in chapter 33, and it looks like he offers forgiveness, although Jacob does not find it easy to accept. But the clearest example is near the end, when Joseph reveals his identity to his brothers, seeking reconciliation (Genesis 45). The brothers only seem to understand their need for forgiveness after their father Jacob has died, when they go to Joseph and say that Jacob left instruction to forgive them. Look at 50:17 to see what they ask.

So at the very end, we finally arrive at actual forgiveness. I wonder whether the story is about how people learned their way towards forgiveness as the right way to handle their broken relationships. What do you think?

People whose faith lies at the heart of their daily lives

Granted all the ways in which they do not get it right, the people of Genesis 12—50 are trying to live lives in God's world and obtain God's blessing. Sometimes it takes a divine intervention to get them back on track, such as when Jacob, on the run from his estranged brother Esau, has a dream of angels going up and down a ladder between heaven and earth (28:12). The dream makes him stop and pray, and it seems to lift him to a new level of commitment. But although there are some spectacular instances of God getting involved directly in the action – talking to Abraham in chapter 18 or wrestling with Jacob in chapter 32 – most of the time God's involvement in the stories is more behind the scenes. What we are watching instead is women and men trying to make their way through life in faithfulness.

How did these people know how to live? The whole story is set before the law was given. But look at 18:17–19 for an interesting passage that raises the possibility that God's standards were already known. You will see at the end of God's speech are the words 'keep the way of the Lord by doing righteousness and justice'.

That phrase – 'doing righteousness and justice' – is more or less exactly what Israel later thinks of as 'keeping the law'. To keep the law is to live this way, in line with the character of God himself. Have a look at Isaiah 33:5 or Jeremiah 9:24 to see the prophets describing God as a God of 'justice and righteousness'. Then look at Isaiah 56:1 or Psalm 106:3 to see how God's people are called to live this way. Look also at the famous verse Isaiah 9:7. Who is the phrase applied to here?

Abraham did not have a specific law to follow, but believing God's promise led him to live in justice and righteousness anyway. The stories of Abraham are not much focused on 'being religious'. They are more about everyday family business than specific acts of worship, prayer or gathering for sacrifices. So we end up with a picture of faithful life as being a matter of everyday issues. Faithfulness is tied up with buying a field, exercising hospitality, choosing a life partner, dividing up property and so forth.

In short, faithfulness is found in everyday trust, in every kind of situation, great or small.

People who only occasionally understand what God is doing

As we read through the stories of Genesis 12—50, it is clear that most of the characters in the story lived without much assurance about what would happen next. This is strongly emphasised right in the opening words, where God says to Abraham, 'Go from your country and your kindred and your father's house to the land that I will show you' (12:1). Abraham does not know where he is to go, but he sets out in faith. We have seen that immediately he starts to make doubtful decisions about the best way to carry out this calling, but first and foremost he is obedient to it, without an awareness of what will happen.

All through the stories, the members of Abraham's extended family struggle to understand what is going on. Abraham is promised many descendants, but has no child, and he is very old before Ishmael is born (17:24). Even then, the story suggests that this birth was engineered by Sarah when she thought there was no chance of any offspring at all (16:2). Then when God promises Sarah her own child, she laughs (18:9–15). Of course, it seems highly unlikely that she would have a child at her age – but that is what happens as the story unfolds. For most of the early part of this story, though, neither Sarah nor Abraham can really see what God is doing or how God is intending to bring about his promise.

Likewise, Jacob travels to and fro – away from his family, back to his family – and worries constantly about who is after him, who is out to get him or what kind of welcome he might receive when he returns. He lives in a world of worry, rather than patient trust.

The question of how we understand God's work in our world is always a difficult one to answer. At the end of the book, after the lengthy story of Joseph surviving all that his brothers did to him and all that he went through in Egypt, the reunited family of brothers is gathered together after the death of their father Jacob. The brothers understandably fear that Joseph may not look kindly on them after all that has happened. Joseph's words at this point are remarkable. Look them up, in Genesis 50:20, and compare them also with his similar words in 45:5–8. How would you summarise what he is saying here?

So the brothers have nothing to fear from Joseph – that is the immediate point of Joseph's words. But the bigger picture that these words point to suggests that God is always at work behind the scenes, bringing the fulfilment of God's purposes even when people are doing their best to disrupt them.

Joseph is able to say this only after experiencing the long years of broken relationships and trouble. At the end, when things have worked out, it becomes possible to look back and see God's hand in what has happened. So 45:5–8 and 50:20 can encourage us that God is always at work. But that does not give us a shortcut to understanding how God is in charge or how to see God's hand in specific circumstances in our own ongoing stories.

5

A theological portrait: what is God's role?

Genesis 12—50 is not just about people; it is about God. That may seem obvious, but sometimes people can read the Bible and think about all sorts of moral or spiritual lessons from it without asking about the God at the centre of it all.

Who is God in Genesis?

The ancient world was full of gods. If you talked about believing in god, the follow-up question would be, 'Which one?' This is a question that makes sense to a lot of people in the 21st century too, especially if they live in multifaith contexts, where competing beliefs are a part of everyday life. For a while in the modern era, many people thought that the word 'God' referred to the one supreme being, who was the same in every religion. Careful readers of the Old Testament will know that it was (and is) more complicated than that.

When referring to God, Genesis varies between using the word that means 'god' (as in 'a god' or 'gods'; the Hebrew word is *'elohim*) and using the proper name of the God of Israel, which was represented in four letters: Y-H-W-H. Scholars suggest that this name was pronounced 'Yahweh', although there is also a tradition of reading it as 'Jehovah'. In truth, we do not know how it was pronounced, partly because Israel never used the name. Out of reverence, they substituted a more general word, meaning 'Lord'. We find this tradition continued in English Bibles, which write 'Lord' instead of YHWH to indicate the name of God.

In Genesis, the name of God is used around 165 times, and the word for 'god' (*'elohim*) around 220 times. This is probably meant to indicate that the God of Israel (YHWH) is the true identity of the 'god' that everyone else talks about, even though everyone else may not know this God in the same way.

Interestingly, Genesis 12—50 includes several other names of God, most of which are unusual or unknown outside these chapters of the Bible. The most famous one is *'el shaddai*, which probably means 'Almighty God'. It occurs half a dozen times. Look at 17:1 for an example. After reappearing in Exodus 6:3, the name occurs only once more in the Bible (in Ezekiel 10:5).

What is important though is this: despite the range of names and words used to talk about God, Genesis is always talking about the one God of Israel, who is the same God we find in the New Testament.

In this guide, and in general when Christians write about Genesis, when we say 'God' we are referring to the one God known in the Old Testament as 'YHWH', who is also called 'the LORD'.

The God who speaks

What does God do in Genesis 12—50? The first thing God does is speak (12:1). In general, and with one intriguing exception, the God of Genesis 12—50 remains in close communication with the key people in the narrative.

You do not have to read far to see God talking to Abraham a lot. Look at 12:1–3, then 12:7, 13:14, 17:1 and so on. Sometimes the wording is different. In chapter 15 we find 'the word of the LORD came to' Abraham. Do you think this means the same thing as 'God said'? The two ways of describing God's speech seem to alternate. Look, for example, at 15:7 in comparison to 15:1. The dialogue between God and Abraham reaches a peak in chapter 22, with the startling story of God asking Abraham to sacrifice Isaac. After this, we do not find God speaking to Abraham again or Abraham talking to God. Is there significance in the communicative silence after such a life-shaking event?

God speaks to Isaac in 26:2–5 and 26:24. As we have said before, Isaac does not have such a major role in the story as his father or his son, and chapter 26 is his main starring chapter.

The focus moves quickly to Jacob, who again is in communication with God. God speaks to Jacob in a dream (28:13–15), but interestingly we do not find Jacob speaking to God directly until 32:9–12, just before the wrestling match in 32:22–32. Jacob is willing to speak about God and to proclaim in God's name (31:53), but there is hardly any focus on Jacob talking to God. What might this tell us about Jacob as a character? God speaks to Jacob in 35:1, 10–12, and Jacob always acknowledges it, but again there is no note of Jacob speaking in reply. Apart from the wrestling match, the nearest we have is Jacob's own account of a dream where he spoke to the angel of God (31:11).

The God of dreams

You will have noticed that alongside the speaking, God appears to Jacob in dreams. This aspect of divine communication moves centre stage in the Joseph story. Remarkably, despite the many long chapters in which God leads and protects Joseph, there is no indication that God speaks to Joseph. Instead, Joseph experiences dreams – indeed his brothers call him 'this dreamer' (37:19), intending it as a negative description. However, Joseph's dreams seem to be the main way that God communicates with him.

There are three main dream incidents, all involving double dreams. The first is in chapter 37, when Joseph has dreams of sheaves of corn and then of stars, and interprets both of them as depicting his brothers (and parents) bowing down to him. The second is in prison in chapter 40, when Joseph hears the dreams of the chief cupbearer and the chief baker, both in prison with him. Joseph offers interpretations that point accurately to what happens: the cupbearer is restored and the baker is hanged. Look at 40:8 to see what Joseph says about these interpretations. This incident is followed immediately by the third pair of dreams (41:1–7), this time Pharaoh's, in which he sees seven thin cows following after seven fat cows and eating them up, and seven thin ears of corn following seven plump and full ears and destroying them. These Joseph interprets both as pointing to seven years of plenty to be followed by seven years of famine (41:25–31). The doubling is interpreted as meaning that 'the thing is fixed by God' (41:32).

Clearly, dream interpretation works for Joseph like God speaking directly works for Abraham and the others. Unlike Jacob's dreams, Joseph's are not about God – God speaks in Jacob's dreams but not Joseph's. However, Joseph's dreams are very much about what God will do.

The book of Genesis does not tell us *why* God communicates with Joseph in dreams. It offers us the picture of Joseph and his dreams, and we watch them working out just as he interprets them, but there is no explanation for this unusual way of hearing from God. Dreams seem to be most prominent in the Old Testament when an Israelite is trying to live faithfully in a non-Israelite context. Joseph and Daniel are the two most notable examples, although there is also an example involving Gideon interpreting a non-Israelite dream (Judges 7:13–15). The key issue seems to be that in dreams God speaks in a way that the non-Israelites can hear without understanding, while Joseph and Daniel are able to grasp the significance. They can do this because they have the wisdom to relate the particular dream to a wider understanding of God's world. This seems to make dreams particularly appropriate for contexts where God's people are surrounded by those who do not know God. The story of Joseph gives us an extended example of this in practice.

The God of covenant

One other aspect of God's communication is that sometimes it takes place in a binding form of speaking known as a 'covenant'. A covenant is like a formal promise, usually committing two parties to a course of action. In Genesis, the two parties are usually God and Abraham, and through Abraham the whole of his descendants. There are also some examples of a covenant between two people: take a look at 21:27, 26:28 and 31:44.

The two main stories about God and Abraham entering into covenant are in chapters 15 and 17. They involve God speaking and Abraham replying. Basically, they involve God's promise to Abraham being spelled out in detail – more descendants than the stars in the sky (15:5); becoming the ancestor of a multitude of nations (17:5), with land commitments too (15:18–21; 17:8) – and then Abraham's commitments in return being spelled out. In chapter 17 this involves the circumcision of male babies. We read that this is 'an everlasting covenant' (17:7).

In the long run, this is a very important way of explaining the God-human relationship. It becomes part of how Jews and Christians think (differently) about God's commitments to us and our obligations in return. As it happens, these issues do not become important in Genesis itself. Abraham does circumcise Isaac 'as God had commanded him' (21:4), but otherwise the covenant or its conditions are not really mentioned. (The only other mentions of circumcision, in chapter 34, do not have much to do with God's promise.) Covenant language becomes much more important when God goes on to make a covenant with Moses in Exodus.

God in human form?

One of the most memorable features of Genesis is when God puts in an appearance in human form. It is not easy to work out whether angelic figures in the narrative are actually an appearance of God. When you read 'the angel of the Lord' speaking, for instance, did that give you the impression that it was God speaking? Many readers think so.

Let's look at the angel of the Lord in Genesis 16 as an example. The angel rescues Hagar after she has been sent away. After this angel has spoken to Hagar in ways that sound a lot like God speaking, what do we read in 16:13? 'So [Hagar] named the Lord who spoke to her, "You are El-roi"' (which means 'God of seeing'). Is it hesitation on the part of the writer(s) about the idea of having Hagar straightforwardly meet God that causes the story to be told so that Hagar meets the angel of the Lord? It certainly seems that, by the end of the chapter, we understand Hagar to have had an encounter with God.

Apart from such angelic interventions, two other stories really stand out as showing God appearing in human form. Both of them use angelic language as part of the difficulty of describing God straight-forwardly interacting with human beings on earth. The first story is Abraham's three visitors at the oaks of Mamre in chapter 18. If you follow the story through, the three people who sit and take afternoon tea with Abraham are described in different ways. In 18:16 they are simply 'the men'. But two of them turn out to be angels (19:1), while the third holds back to talk to Abraham about what is about to unfold in Sodom. Who does this third character turn out to be? Take a look at 18:17.

The intense dialogue that follows sees Abraham arguing with God, trying to secure justice for any righteous people to be found in Sodom. His famous plea/prayer is: 'Shall not the Judge of all the earth do what is just?' (18:25). He argues God down from saving the city for the sake of 50 righteous people, to saving it for ten righteous people. Perhaps he stopped at ten because he thought there would be that many, or perhaps he thought it secured his nephew Lot and his own family, or perhaps it has something to do with ten people being enough to make up a righteous gathering of faithful people. In any case, the city is destroyed, and only Lot and his two daughters make it out alive.

Why would this story be told about God himself, rather than an angel? Is it because the only way to make sense of such judgement is to have it as an act of God himself? In other words – if this were an angel or just an outcome of warfare, the question would always be what God thought of it. But chapters 18—19 leave no room for doubt: God inflicted this punishment on the city. That does not make it an easy or satisfying story. But it does leave the point clear, by involving God personally in the action.

The same might be said about the other divine appearance in human form, in the wrestling match with Jacob in 32:22–32. We will look at this story later.

When God is not directly intervening in the narrative, this does not mean that he is not involved. More commonly, God's interaction is through 'supervising' events from a distance. In the Joseph story, as we saw earlier, this is a kind of behind-the-scenes supervision, and God's action only becomes clear in retrospect (see 50:20 again). However it happens – hands-on or from afar – Genesis 12—50 is a God-focused narrative throughout. Yes, it is a story about people. But it is always, at the same time, a story about God.

6

A historical setting: what is the relationship with history?

So far, we have been reading the stories of Genesis 12—50 at face value and learning about the people and the God that we find there. Everything we have said is about the picture that Genesis 12—50 paints for us. Since that is the picture that scripture gives us, it is a good idea to spend time appreciating it in all its delicate and deliberate detail.

However, there is another kind of question that readers can ask: how does all this match up to what happened? In what way, if any, is Genesis 12—50 like a history book? We may also have questions about who wrote it and when, and what the book was originally trying to do in the ancient world. All of these are historical questions in one way or another. In this section, we explore these issues a little.

I have to start with a potentially disappointing warning: all of this took place a long time ago and in a 'galaxy' (the ancient Near East) far, far away. Much of the time our answer to historical questions is going to be, 'We do not know.' Sometimes, though, these questions can still lead to useful perspectives, so it can be worth asking them. I will organise this discussion around four particular questions that often attract people's attention.

Who wrote Genesis 12—50?

We do not know. The author of Genesis 12—50 is lost in the mists of time.

There is a long-standing tradition that Moses wrote Genesis. Indeed, in German for instance, the names of the first five books of the Bible are '1 Moses', '2 Moses', etc. So that would certainly make it easy to assume that Moses wrote it. But the point of those names is to emphasise what everyone has always said – whether or not they are German – that these are 'the five books of Moses': Genesis to Deuteronomy. This is correct, but is not actually a claim about who wrote them. The same is true, for example, of a book like Ruth, which is called 'Ruth' because it is about Ruth, not written by Ruth.

There is nothing in the books themselves to suggest that Moses wrote them, and quite a lot to suggest he did not. For example, when Moses is written about it is always as 'he' and not 'I'. And Genesis takes place before Moses' birth, while Deuteronomy ends after his death.

The real point about the tradition of 'the five books of Moses' is that they have authority as the foundational books of Jewish (and then Christian) scripture. You will see as you look through the Old Testament that we usually do not know who wrote down the books, but this does not stop them from being understandable and important. The New Testament never links the book of Genesis to any particular author. It was not an important question in biblical times to know who wrote Genesis, and so no answer to this question was preserved.

This has not stopped a lot of theories about who wrote Genesis. One widespread theory is based on the different names of God that are used, which we looked at in the previous section (YHWH, *'elohim*, etc.). Many scholars suggest that different authors wrote different sections, and that we can distinguish them depending on which name of God is used. Their idea was that different sections come from the documents of different traditions, and so this is known as 'the Documentary hypothesis'. This is a plausible theory, but whoever edited the whole book of Genesis together did such a good job that most of us will be better off just reading Genesis as it stands rather than worrying too much about where its individual sections came from.

When was Genesis 12—50 written?

Again: we do not know. Different stories may well come from different times, over a long period. My own guess is that such stories circulated in oral tradition for a long time, being passed down in family traditions, told to the children, recited at gatherings and so on. Probably some written versions of the stories then developed, until eventually people put together these written stories into the complete book of Genesis. There are a wide range of guesses for when this process happened, and most likely it happened in stages over a period of time. Perhaps the book of Genesis was finished quite late in the history of ancient Israel. People have guessed at any time between the 10th and 6th centuries BC for the final edit, and there is little chance of being more precise.

One interesting question is why the characters we read about in Genesis 12—50 are not often referred to in later books of the Old Testament. Whereas Moses is constantly mentioned in later books, Abraham and co are not a big focus of attention. Take a look at Psalm 105 to see how it tells a short version of the story of Abraham and of Joseph on its way to talking about Moses and Aaron and the exodus. In fact, this is really quite unusual in the Old Testament. This psalm is basically the only psalm that mentions Joseph (as a person, rather than a name for the people), and Psalm 105:9 is the only mention of Isaac in the Psalms. Maybe the Genesis stories were simply not so well known through much of Israel's history. Or maybe the general life stories they tell, which make them so interesting to us, were thought to be less helpful for explaining life under the law of Moses or under the king.

In any case, these stories have a low profile in the rest of the Old Testament, and one result is that we have almost no indication of when they were written down.

What is the historical setting of Genesis 12—50?

This is a much more helpful question, in the sense that it looks at what is in the book and asks about how to make sense of that in historical terms. In other words, this is a historical question about the world that we encounter in reading Genesis 12—50, rather than a historical question about the world that produced the written book of Genesis.

In general terms, the ancestral world of Genesis 12—50 fits with what we know from the early or middle second millennium BC, that is, between 2000BC and anywhere up to and beyond 1500BC. Immediately following the book of Genesis is the story of the exodus from Egypt, and there has been a long attempt to find an approximate date when that occurred. This is hard to do, because we are not sure which Pharaoh is being talked about in Exodus or how to read some of the passages about dates that probably use symbolic numbers (e.g. '40 years' probably means 'a long time', and multiples of 40 years, such as '480 years' (12 x 40), probably mean a really long time). But our best guesses put the exodus in either the 15th or 13th century BC. That means that the Abraham-to-Joseph stories are in the time before that period.

The key cultural point about the stories, at least in chapters 12—38, is that they depict a nomadic way of life, with settlements in small local areas and a lot of moving around. This makes very good sense for the world at this stage. There is very little structure, in terms of cities or temples (or tabernacles). A city was probably a settlement that had endured for a while. This changes when the story moves to Egypt in chapter 39, and we encounter a much more developed civilisation.

Worship could take place wherever people encountered God, and altars were often erected in honour of God. Abraham starts this tradition early. Look at 12:7–8 to see how straightforwardly he does it. Other striking examples include Isaac building an altar at Beer-sheba when God appears to him (26:25) and Jacob erecting an altar on a 'plot of land' in the 'city of Shechem' (33:20). What is interesting about these incidents is that later in Israel's history there was a strong emphasis on sacrificing only at the divinely given central locations: the tabernacle (Leviticus 17:3–4) and in due course the temple (see Deuteronomy 12:1–7). Although in practice a lot of other altars were used, they were seen as less than ideal, whereas in Genesis 12—50 this more relaxed approach is common and is not condemned.

Geographically, these chapters start from the far east, in ancient Mesopotamia, a name that means 'between two rivers', which were the Tigris and the Euphrates. These flow down through what is modern-day Iraq, all the way to the Persian Gulf. Look at 11:31: Abraham was part of the family that set out from Ur, which was quite near the Persian Gulf, and made their way to Haran, a long way north-west from there, on the way to the land of Canaan. Most of the remaining stories then take place in and around Canaan and to the north of that land, especially as Jacob travels around between the family home in Canaan and the home of his uncle Laban, in Haran (27:43), back where Abraham had first settled.

Are the stories of Genesis 12—50 historically accurate?

This question is difficult to answer. Very simply, we have no way of knowing. There is no specific evidence against which we can measure the stories, so there is nothing to fact check them against. The above section on historical setting shows that the stories make a lot of sense in the world of the ancient Near East as we know it. Place names are generally recognisable, and the customs make sense. So the stories are historically plausible. But there are a few reasons for being cautious about saying more than this.

First, it is clear that some verses in Genesis do presuppose a good period of time between the events described and when the book is written down. Examples of this include references like 'At that time the Canaanites were in the land' (12:6), which shows that they were gone before this was written, suggesting that someone has written – or edited – this story after the time of Joshua. For another example, take a look at 36:31. What part of later Israelite history does this assume? Neither of these references demonstrate anything about accuracy, but they show that there was a very long time period during which the book was being compiled. This is one reason to be cautious about its status as historical reporting.

A second reason to be cautious is that historical reporting was not the point of the stories in Genesis 12—50. In the ancient world, it was important to tell stories faithfully, but 'faithfully' meant reliably communicating the key issues. In other words, it makes sense to say that the stories of Genesis 12—50 are reliable in what they are trying to say, but it does not seem likely that one of the things they were trying to say was, 'This is exactly what happened.' This puts the stories somewhere between 'history' and 'story', as those labels are used today. I think the best option is to say that they are 'history-like' stories, but more importantly that they are truthful (reliable and faithful) stories. In other words, they successfully communicate whatever their ancient authors and editors wanted to communicate, such as the truth about God and how God interacts with people. On the whole, this did not include questions of being historically accurate in our modern sense.

A good example of how little we know about historical accuracy, and how little it helps us understand the stories anyway, is the repeated example of God speaking. When we read, '[God] said, "Take your son, your only son Isaac…"' (22:2), or that the Lord said to Isaac, 'I am the God of your father Abraham' (26:24), do we imagine an audible voice? Or an inner conviction in Abraham and Isaac that this is what God wants? Or an inner experience of a voice saying those words? It makes good sense to say that these stories are faithfully capturing what Abraham and Isaac understood God to be communicating with them, but beyond that we neither know nor need to know exactly what happened.

A historical imagination

Having spent most of this section saying, 'We do not know' or 'We cannot say', I want to end on a more positive note. There are two great benefits of thinking carefully about historical questions. First, we are forced to pay attention to details in the biblical text and take them seriously, which is always a good thing. Second, understanding these details helps to inform our imaginations, which helps us to read more thoughtfully. The more we know about how the world of the time worked, the more likely we are to spot what is important or what matters in the story. Historical background helps get us into the world where the real story takes place. That is why we need it: as a step towards our imaginative engagement with the story being told.

Think of it like a TV production crew doing the background research to get the story of an ancient figure (e.g. Jesus or Julius Caesar) historically appropriate. They would feel disappointed if your response to the finished drama was, 'But is it historically accurate?' They would have achieved their goal if your response was, 'What a powerful story!', because you had been enabled to make sense of the story despite its unusual historical details.

7

Some key passages

In this section, we look at a few key passages in a bit more detail. Have your Bible open ready to look at the specifics. I have picked three different kinds of passage.

1 Texts of promise

Genesis 12:1–3

The opening of Genesis 12—50 is a remarkable one. God speaks to Abraham and sets in motion a project of blessing that will last for the whole of the rest of the Bible, extending even to 'all the families of the earth'. What exactly does this little passage say?

First comes the command to go. Usually translated just as 'Go', verse 1 begins with a phrase more like 'Get yourself off from/to…' that we otherwise find only in chapter 22 (see below). I sometimes try to capture it with, 'Get up and go!' Abraham has to leave his homeland, his people and his father's house – in other words, leave behind everything he knows. He is not even told where he is going; it is to the land that God will show him.

Then comes the promise that God will make of him a great nation. Abraham's age at this point is unknown, but it will become clear as we read on that there is a simple and single problem in the way of this promise: Abraham is getting old and has no children. It will take several chapters to untangle this problem, and the ways that Abraham and Sarah try to fix it do not help.

But not only is he promised a nation, that is, offspring; Abraham is also told that God will bless him and that he – Abraham – will be a blessing. The theme of blessing runs all the way through Genesis 12—50. To bless is to bring God's favour upon someone, so of course in one sense only God can bless. But here God is tying that blessing to the person of Abraham. More specifically, what does it mean for Abraham to 'be a blessing'? In Hebrew, this phrase means that the person in question (Abraham) lives a life that points people to God as the source of blessing. In other words, it is not just what Abraham might say but everything he does that draws people towards receiving God's favour.

The blessing then overflows in verse 3: God promises to bless those who bless Abraham, and correspondingly to curse those who curse him (or perhaps more precisely, those who 'dishonour' him, as the ESV puts it). Then at the climax of this amazing multiple-level promise, God says, 'In you all the families of the earth shall be blessed'. It is a little hard to translate this final word. In 26:4 this promise is recalled, and the wording there says that they 'shall gain blessing for themselves'. So it is clearly about blessing, but maybe it has the sense of others being blessed when they look at Abraham and see how God blesses him. That is what I mean by 'the blessing overflows'.

In its context, this is one man, with his immediate family, striking out into a vast wilderness, a long way from home. Just getting through the day would be an achievement. So to be told that he will do much more than survive – that people will watch him go and find a blessing from the God of Abraham in doing so – is a remarkable encouragement.

Jewish readers are delighted, and rightly so, that 'Father Abraham' is given such a magnificent promise in these opening moments of his story. His name has indeed become great, greater than just this one faith tradition, as millions of people in Christian and

Islamic traditions also look back to Abraham. In one sense, all God's work in human history from this point on flows from this promise.

Christian readers have seen a further overflowing blessing. Christians sometimes think of themselves as more like all those other 'families of the earth', who have been blessed in and through Abraham. As God's mission has gone out through the life of the church over the past 2,000 years, there is hardly a place on earth that has not been touched by God's blessing activity. So in this sense, all the work of Christian mission can also look back to Genesis 12 and see how it flows from this promise.

The promise is repeated more than once in Genesis. Although the precise wording of the promise varies, have a look at:

- 18:18 – God reflecting to himself about Abraham
- 22:18 – an angel of the Lord echoing the promise once more to Abraham
- 26:4 – God talking to Isaac
- 28:14 – God talking to Jacob in a dream.

One reason why God is known as 'the God of Abraham, Isaac and Jacob', may be because he makes this promise to these three people.

The family story that follows chapter 12 shows clearly how fragile this promise seemed, over and over, as the extended family went about its business. It rarely looked as if a great nation was taking shape. Perhaps without the powerful words of 12:1–3 the family would have lost heart entirely.

Genesis 48—49

We saw earlier that by the end of chapter 50, the status of God's promise to Abraham has been reduced to the bones of Joseph in a box. But just before this downbeat ending, there are two chapters that almost serve as a trailer for what is to come. Jacob, who is known as 'Israel' in this story, is dying, and Joseph and his two sons, Manasseh and Ephraim, come to meet him. They will now be part of his inheritance (48:5).

Jacob blesses them but switches his hands so that the stronger blessing goes to the younger son, Ephraim (48:19). In due course, the tribe of Ephraim would become the largest of the northern tribes of

Israel – sometimes the whole northern kingdom would simply be known as 'Ephraim'.

Chapter 49 then includes Jacob's farewell words to his twelve sons. In 49:28, we read that in so doing 'he blessed them, blessing each one of them with a suitable blessing'. The order in which he blesses them is not the same as the order they are introduced earlier in the book, but it does begin with the first four sons, by Leah, and end with the last two, by Rachel: Joseph and Benjamin.

Much of what Jacob says here can be matched up to the later stories of the tribes descended from the sons. Levi, for instance, becomes the priestly tribe, with no land allocation of its own (see 49:7). Look in particular at the blessing of Judah, the fourth son (49:8–12). This is the most positive of all the blessings, matched only by the one given to Joseph. The particular promise to Judah in 49:10 suggests that there will always be royal power attached to the tribe of Judah. Jewish readers see this fulfilled in King David, of the tribe of Judah. Christian readers trace the line further, to Jesus, the 'Lion of the tribe of Judah' (Revelation 5:5).

By including these promises near the end of the book, chapter 49 shows that the promise to Abraham is alive and well. It may look precarious at this point, and it will be a long time before the fulfilment becomes clear. But somehow this strange narrative of struggles to have children – and then scheming between parents, maidservants and sons – has ended up producing a family of twelve sons which will grow into the twelve tribes of Israel. The God of Genesis 12—50 is a God who keeps promises.

2 Texts of mystery

Genesis 22

'After these things God tested Abraham.' So begins one of the most remarkable and mysterious stories of the Bible, even by its own extraordinary standards. The shocking tale of chapter 22 sees God tell Abraham to take his son Isaac – called his 'only son' here because he is the long-awaited child of the promise through whom all the blessings are supposed to work out – to Moriah and 'offer him there as a burnt-offering'. The idea of God asking for child sacrifice is terrifying, and the reader is only partly protected from the shock by reading in verse 1 that this is a 'test'. And remember that Abraham does not know that.

The story is worth reading slowly and carefully, and you should turn to it now and read through it alongside these notes. You will be struck by the building tension: the repeated 'So the two of them walked on together' (verses 6 and 8) – towards Isaac's doom? – and Abraham's repeated use of a single Hebrew word, which translates as 'Here I am!', a kind of acknowledgement of readiness for whatever is next:

- He says it to God at the beginning (v. 1).
- He says it to Isaac as they arrive at the sacrifice site (v. 7).
- He says it to the angel of the Lord as the angel intervenes at what seems the last possible moment (v. 11).

And then in verse 12, at last, the command to stand down, as Isaac's life is saved and an alternative sacrifice provided. Abraham names the place 'The Lord will provide' – using words that play on the idea that 'providing' and 'seeing' ('provision' and 'vision') are part of the way that God gets involved in the situation.

The awfulness and intensity of this test have provoked many readers down the centuries to recognise that something unusual is happening here. The 'test' seems to be about Abraham's willingness to give up everything for God, rather than actually being an attempt to raise the possibility of child sacrifice (which was condemned in Israel, in due course). This is the way Jewish tradition has understood it: that Abraham survives the ultimate test here and in so doing models what it means to have the deepest faith imaginable.

One detail of the story certainly points this way. The story begins with the unusual phrase 'Get yourself up and go!' (the 'go' of verse 2), which we saw only comes elsewhere in 12:1. It highlights that both these stories involve setting off in faith towards an unclear future. There, Abraham was being told to go to the land that God would show him, but here, he is told where the place to go is: the land of Moriah (v. 2). This place is only named one other time in the Bible, in 2 Chronicles 3:1, where it is given as the site of the temple that Solomon is starting to build. In other words, chapter 22 takes place on what would become the temple site. Does this suggest that Abraham provides an example here of precisely what the point of the temple was – to offer to God all that we have, and in the process to receive back from God the blessing of life?

The temple and its sacrifices were not always understood in this life-giving way, just as the story of Abraham is not always understood in this life-giving way.

It is, of course, possible to be so shocked by it that we miss the point. But reading it as a modern psychological drama, and trying for example to imagine how Abraham would feel, is to treat the story as something it is not. You might have noticed in reading it through that the story says nothing about emotions or inner thoughts at all. The story is not told for that reason. But it is told to tell us about a 'test': a test of faith that points to what it means to offer everything to God.

Genesis 32:22–32

If chapter 22 is mysterious and shocking, this story is just completely mysterious. Jacob, en route to reunite with his brother Esau and considerably worried about that reunion, finds himself alone at night at a ford on the Jabbok river. His wives, household and possessions have gone on ahead. It is just him – alone in the dark, awaiting the moment of truth next day.

Then 'a man wrestled with him until daybreak' (v. 24). What becomes clear, or rather remains unclear, is that we never find out who this 'man' is. Even more, the story sticks with saying 'he' when we cannot work out which 'he' it is: Jacob or this other man. The other man puts out Jacob's hip socket, apparently by some mysteriously powerful touch (v. 25), which seems to be triggered by the experience of not being able to win in a fair fight. Then, as the sun starts to come up, the strange man asks Jacob to let him go.

Jacob will not let him go without a blessing. He appears to get one eventually (at the end of v. 29), although it is unclear exactly what this involves. The story seems more interested in talking about names: Jacob wants to know who he has been wrestling, and there are two incidents of renaming.

First, the strange man renames Jacob as 'Israel' (v. 28). He says this is because 'you have striven with God and with humans' – or divine and human beings. The word 'Israel' does not actually mean that; if anything, it means 'God strives' or more likely 'God rules'. Having asked for a blessing and received a name, Jacob switches to asking for a name – 'Who are you?' – and receives a blessing (v. 29). He never gets the attacker's name, but in verse 30 he renames the place 'Peniel', which can mean 'face of God', which Jacob then explains is because – in his view – he has indeed met with God.

The sun rises. Jacob limps. There is a strange verse about food laws arising from this story – which feels like quite an anticlimax and is understood in Jewish tradition as being attached to the story later once the food laws in general came in.

In one sense, Jacob has had a long, dark night of the soul. But it is not just his 'inner demons' that he is wrestling. The story is clear that there is a genuine opponent and physical damage. The traditional view is that Jacob is wrestling an angel. This tradition is already found in Hosea 12:4–5. Whether we can read more into it than that, such as whether the angelic presence is somehow at the same time the presence of God, is again unclear.

One thing is clear, though: Jacob is renamed Israel in this context of wrestling with God (whether through an angel or not). The emphasis on naming in the story points to it telling us about what it means to be 'Israel'. Later, Israelites are invited to see this as part of their self-understanding: they are a people who wrestle with God, who find that the God who blesses them also at times stands in their way. Jacob's limp may be a reminder to people of faith: progress in life with God can be complex, costly and, above all, mysterious.

3 Texts of terror

There is so much to say in a short guide to Genesis 12—50 that most of our time has been taken up with the major figures and stories that are part of the development of the promise to Abraham and its fulfilment. But it is genuinely striking how much space is given in Genesis to other characters, to darker stories and to portraits of loss and disaster.

The phrase 'texts of terror' can point to some of these powerful but disturbing narratives. The fact that they are in the Bible is important. The experiences they describe are not forgotten and not airbrushed out to make a story where everything always works out well. In other words, even texts of terror can offer hope to those who have experienced terror. God has not forgotten them.

Often in Genesis, such stories involve women. We said earlier how the book gives an unexpected focus to women in its narrative: Sarah and Rebekah are every bit as complex as Abraham and Isaac, in good and bad ways, and we could explore their own struggles and sufferings just as much. We also find women treated in cruel ways, and not just by men. The difficulties experienced by Hagar in chapter 16 come partly from

Sarah and partly from what the angel of the Lord says. But often the problems are caused by men. I offer brief comments on just three examples.

Genesis 19

After God and Abraham have wrangled over how many righteous people might save Sodom, and it turns out that there were not enough of them, two angels turn up in Sodom to bring about its destruction. Lot invites them to stay in his house, but his house is then attacked by the men of Sodom, who want to have sex with the guests.

The real moment of terror arrives with Lot's reply to this situation. Effectively, he offers his two virgin daughters to the mob instead (v. 8). Lot does not emerge as a hero from any of his actions in Genesis, although this negative judgement is in tension with the way he is remembered as 'righteous' in the New Testament (2 Peter 2:7). As we read on, it is of some relief to see that the two angelic visitors intervene and actually stop the daughters being taken by the mob.

The disarray of Lot's extended family is hinted at in the rest of the story (look at the attitude of his sons-in-law-to-be in verse 14), and his relationship with his daughters ends in shame too (vv. 30–38). Genesis uses this last story to explain the origin of two peoples who would always be enemies to Israel: the Moabites and the Ammonites.

What may be most shocking about chapter 19 is the way the story of Lot and his daughters is told without apparent condemnation of Lot's words in verse 8. The violent visitors are clearly condemned, but not Lot. We are left to watch the negative implications of what he has done unfold gradually. But this is typical of most Old Testament narrative, which as we have said often refuses to give evaluation.

Genesis 21

This chapter begins with celebration: Sarah finally bears Abraham the promised son, Isaac, and there is thankfulness and rejoicing (up to verse 8). But Sarah turns against Ishmael, Hagar's son, almost immediately. Sarah asks Abraham to cast Ishmael out, which distresses Abraham.

The story turns darker with the words of God given in verses 12–13. God tells Abraham to do whatever

Sarah wants, since the promised offspring will come through Isaac. God's apparent lack of interest in Ishmael is tempered by adding that a nation will also come from Ishmael, but this does not stop Abraham sending Hagar and Ishmael out into the desert with not enough to survive. The harrowing story then follows of Hagar's supplies running out in the heat, and she lies down to die.

Once again, there is divine intervention at the last moment: an angel of God leads her to a well and passes on to Hagar the news about Ishmael's descendants that, until then, only Abraham had heard.

More than once in the book, Hagar has her life put in jeopardy and her own cares and concerns ignored. The picture this gives us of human relationships, even among God's people, is a sobering one. On the one hand, it stands as a warning for later readers. On the other, there may be some encouragement for readers who think their own life experience is like Hagar's. Such experiences cannot be explained or justified, but they do not fall entirely outside God's care.

Genesis 38

A final 'text of terror' concerns Judah, who has three
sons: Er, Onan and Shelah (vv. 3–5). Er marries Tamar,
but Er dies, and then the expectation is that one of Er's
brothers will marry – and thus care for – Tamar. Onan
effectively refuses and dies, and then Shelah, when
he finally grows up, is not given to her either (v. 14).

So Tamar apparently disguises herself as a prostitute
(according to verse 21), and fools her father-in-law
Judah into sleeping with her. She takes proof of his
identity. She also becomes pregnant.

When Judah hears his daughter-in-law is pregnant, he
wants her put to death (v. 24), at which point Tamar
provides the proof that it is her father-in-law who is
responsible for it. Strangely, the story suggests that
Judah thinks she has done the right thing. Once again,
this tale of the casual mistreatment of family, and in
particular of women, is simply left to bear its startling
witness. Readers of Genesis might learn: do not pretend all is well when it is not; do not be crushed by
failings, but learn from them; and do not suppose that
being blessed by God means you will not act badly.

8

What about that amazing technicolour dreamcoat?

I am aware as we have gone through the book that we have spent more time on Abraham, Isaac and Jacob, and their extended families, than we have on Joseph. We have not ignored Joseph completely – we looked at his dreams and his powerful statement of trust in God (50:20). But the Joseph narrative is one long story, set in a different part of the world from the earlier chapters, and it is hard to do justice to it in a short guide to Genesis.

Fortunately, as I mentioned at the beginning, there is a wonderful modern musical on hand to introduce you to the story in detail: Tim Rice and Andrew Lloyd Webber's *Joseph and the Amazing Technicolour Dreamcoat*. It basically tells you the story of chapters 37 and 39—50, with a degree of imagination, leaving out some genealogies and some technical details about Egyptian government administration, but adding in Pharaoh as Elvis Presley and some upbeat choreography. All in all, most people would probably take that as a good deal, even if Bible scholars get nervous when people make any changes to the story.

As it happens, one slightly complicated issue in interpreting the Joseph story concerns what kind of coat he was wearing. The word that describes the coat occurs three times (37:3, 23, 32), and the traditional English translation – in the KJV – is 'coat of many colours'. Modern English translations often do not say this. The NRSV says 'long robe with sleeves' while others say 'ornate robe' (NIV) or 'elaborately embroidered/fancy coat' (MSG). What is going on here?

It must have been quite some coat. That is obvious because it is precisely the reason why the brothers are annoyed with him: this coat (or robe) is a sign of favouritism, so it is special in some way. The Hebrew word that describes the coat on these three occasions in chapter 37 is *pas* (in fact, the plural form, *passim*), and one guess we have for this unusual word is that it means 'long-sleeved'. The only other place this word occurs is in 2 Samuel 13:18–19, where it refers to a noteworthy robe worn by the 'virgin daughters of the king' in Israel – and we have the same range of options for understanding it there.

Some scholars say that similar phrases in other languages point to it meaning 'richly ornamented'. A Jewish tradition suggests the word is related to the word for the palm of the hand or the sole of the foot – the idea being that the robe reaches down to the hand and foot, hence 'long robe with sleeves'.

When the Bible was translated into Greek, probably around the 3rd century BC in the case of Genesis, this description became *poikilos*, which does indeed mean 'many coloured'. Since it was in Greek (or Latin) that the Bible was mainly read for hundreds of years, you can see why the KJV translated it 'coat of many colours'. My own view is that this is still a perfectly good translation, even if we cannot be sure just how bright this richly ornamented/long-sleeved robe would have been.

In a story of such vivid characterisation and larger-than-life moments, I actually think that the phrase 'amazing technicolour dreamcoat' does a wonderful job of capturing just how remarkable this robe was and just what sort of envious feelings it provoked in the brothers. So my vote is to stick with the title.

But a more wide-ranging issue about the modern musical version of the Joseph story might be worth considering. We looked earlier at how God withdraws from direct involvement in the Genesis narrative when we get to the Joseph story, at least in his involvement with Joseph personally. Joseph – you will recall – meets God by way of having dreams, but not in the dreams themselves and not in direct speech. So it is certainly possible to tell the Joseph story without God as an active character in the narrative, and the musical version does this.

What is different is that in the musical God more or less stops being present at all. God's speech to Jacob in chapter 46 is not included, though this could be for perfectly fair dramatic reasons. But the idea that Pharaoh's double dream underlines the certainty that God will act is turned into there not being any doubt 'what your dreams are all about'. Probably the biggest change is in the twice-repeated song, used in part as the finale of the musical, that 'any dream will do'. We are no longer looking at dreams as God's communication with Joseph, but dreams as a kind of aspirational image for making the most of what life brings you. I am sure that is not the worst thing to wish for anybody, but neither does it have much to do with Genesis and its story of Joseph.

Needless to say, the pointed declaration that Joseph makes in 50:20, to which we have referred several times already, also fades from sight. I do not want the point of this section to be that a piece of musical theatre is first and foremost to be judged by all the ways it deviates from the biblical text. That would be a strange way of ever expecting to enjoy musical theatre. It would also be a poor way to honour the importance of using our imaginations when we read the Bible. Nevertheless, it is still worth making sure that after we have enjoyed the musical, and even defended its title, that our theology comes instead from the version found in the Bible, even when we read it with full imaginative engagement.

In any case, there is also so much more in the Joseph story than can be captured in a two-hour performance. What might we learn about life as a refugee from seeing how Joseph is treated, his name changed into something unrecognisable by Pharaoh (41:45) and his whole life diverted into working for a foreign government, a long way from his own home and familiar life? Stories like those of Joseph may be especially relevant to us in the 21st century, in an age of massive international upheaval and of people needing to learn faithful living 'in exile'.

What better place to end than with Joseph's words that we have looked at before, which more or less bring the book of Genesis itself to a close: 'Even though you intended to do harm to me, God intended it for good, in order to preserve a numerous people, as he is doing today' (50:20). Those words were written thousands of years ago, but it is still 'today' and the same God is still at work, in the same life-giving ways.

So let us take and read Genesis 12—50 – enter into its story – attentive to the literary, theological and historical details, but most of all letting our imaginations engage with the world that Genesis lays out before us. Happy reading.

9

Questions for reflection or discussion

1 What has surprised you about Genesis 12—50?

2 What have you learned from Genesis 12—50 about how God's people relate to God? And vice versa: how God relates to God's people?

3 How has reading Genesis 12—50 shaped your spiritual life? How could its stories and characters affect the way in which you look for God's involvement in your daily life?

4 How would you encourage others to read this book?

5 If you had to choose the three most important stories from Genesis 12—50, which would they be? Why?

6   How has understanding Genesis 12—50 helped
    you grasp the overall story of the Bible more
    clearly?

7   What particular aspects of modern living can be
    related to the situations addressed in the stories
    of Abraham and his extended family?

8   How could the stories of Genesis 12—50 be used
    to reach out to people with the gospel message?

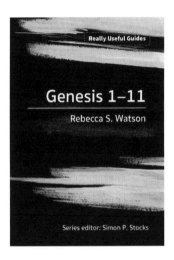

This Really Useful Guide to Genesis 1—11 opens up afresh what can be a familiar text. In showing us how to engage with these stories, Rebecca S. Watson gives us background information about how, why and when Genesis was written, tips for reading and studying, and a summary of how Genesis 1—11 fits into the biblical story.

Really Useful Guides: Genesis 1—11

Rebecca S. Watson

978 0 85746 791 1 £5.99

brfonline.org.uk

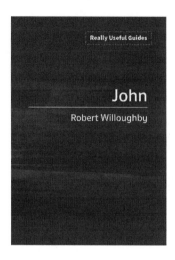

This Really Useful Guide to John gives practical tips on how to open up this rich gospel. Robert Willoughby offers clear explanations of John's signs, 'I am' sayings and recurring images, alongside unpacking its themes and significance. Full of digestible wisdom and overflowing with enthusiasm, this book will ultimately draw you closer to Jesus.

Really Useful Guides: John
Robert Willoughby
978 0 85746 751 5 £5.99

brfonline.org.uk

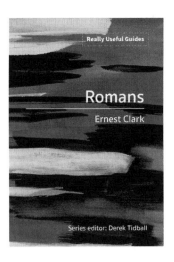

This Really Useful Guide to Romans covers many helpful aspects of the letter, from its intended recipients to its central themes. Emphasising that this is a message of grace and good news to God's loved ones as well as a profound theological treatise, he goes on to look at how Romans fits alongside other New Testament writings and what it means for us as believers today.

Really Useful Guides: Romans
Ernest Clark
978 0 85746 822 2 £5.99

brfonline.org.uk

Enabling all ages to grow in faith

Anna Chaplaincy
Living Faith
Messy Church
Parenting for Faith

100 years of BRF

2022 is BRF's 100th anniversary! Look out for details of our special new centenary resources, a beautiful centenary rose and an online thanksgiving service that we hope you'll attend. This centenary year we're focusing on sharing the story of BRF, the story of the Bible – and we hope you'll share your stories of faith with us too.

Find out more at **brf.org.uk/centenary**.

To find out more about our work, visit
brf.org.uk

Sharing
the Story
since 1922